FIRE OF LOVE

The Spirituality of John Wesley

FIRE OF LOVE

The Spirituality of John Wesley

GORDON WAKEFIELD

Darton, Longman and Todd

First Published in Great Britain in 1976 by
Darton, Longman and Todd Ltd
85 Gloucester Road, London SW7 4SU
© 1976 Gordon Wakefield

ISBN 0 232 51357 0

Printed in Great Britain by
The Anchor Press Ltd and bound by
Wm Brendon & Son Ltd
both of Tiptree, Essex

CONTENTS

PART ONE

Introduction

JOHN WESLEY

It was a Sunday morning in May 1742. The little clergyman was in Newcastle upon Tyne and at seven o'clock he stood with a companion at a street corner in Sandgate, 'the poorest and most contemptible part of the town'. His hair was smooth and well-brushed, his bands immaculately white, his shoes buckled. He began to sing the hundredth Psalm. Faces appeared at windows and soon people were on the streets, in twos and threes at first, but then in dozens. He ceased singing and started to tell them of the one, who was 'wounded for our transgressions and bruised for our iniquities'. By the time he had done there were over a thousand people, very quiet, almost motionless, 'gaping and staring with profound astonishment'. They had never seen such a parson before. The clergy belonged to the churches, not the slums; and the manner and tone of voice were for most of the time those of cultured society, with an occasional note of vehemence, passion and direct appeal. He said 'If you desire to know who I am, my name is John Wesley. At five in the evening, with God's help, I design to preach here again'.

It was not always like that as Wesley travelled the country. At Leominster he made a tombstone in the churchyard his pulpit, but the crowd was noisy and they rang the bells to drown his voice. His clear words surmounted the clangour until the organ joined in, whereupon he removed to the corn-market and addressed an even larger company undisturbed.

Sometimes the town ruffians, often enough inflamed by drink, set upon him and dispersed his hearers, but he sustained little injury and was never deterred. Sometimes the crowds seethed and there was a sound like the sea and the waves roaring, and in his presence people fell into fits and foamed at the mouth as though demons inside them were putting up a last fight at the onslaught of supernatural goodness. When calmed, they acknowledged themselves changed persons and nearly always joined the group of followers Wesley left behind, who came to be called 'Methodists'. By the time he died, in 1791, there were 70,000 of them in Britain and 15,000 in America.

What is remarkable about his movement is that it represents the confluence of his own spiritual experience with the uninhibited 'folk' religion, which he aroused and directed. He made the working people of the first industrial revolution free of the spirituality of the Christian ages, though they clothed it in cultural forms which have disguised it from much of Christendom. Rather in spite of himself, Wesley fathered a riotous Christianity, but its adherents were turned from the streets to the chapels and taught to seek social reform in constitutional and non-violent ways.

Wesley's Spiritual Pilgrimage

John Wesley was born in 1703, the sixteenth child of the Rector of Epworth, Samuel Wesley, and his wife, Susanna. The two were themselves children of ministers who had been ejected from the Church of England because they could not conform to the Book of Common Prayer after the

Restoration of Charles II. But they had returned to the Church in their young adulthood as orthodox dissent drifted into unitarianism. The home, in the somewhat barbarous fenland of the Isle of Axholme, was Puritan and Prayer-Book too. The Bible was at its heart, but Susanna in particular sympathised with later nonconformists of a different kind, the 'non-jurors' as they are more precisely called, those Anglicans who could not accept the religious settlement of 1689. There was, therefore, a touch of the old, non-Roman, non-ritualistic high churchmanship, strong for the legal state connection and strict about prayer and fasting.

When Wesley was six years old, the rectory at Epworth was destroyed by fire. The small boy was almost forgotten in the confusion and was rescued by a servant even as his absent-minded father was kneeling down to give thanks for the deliverance of all his family. Jackie was taken straight to his mother and he and she always saw a special Providence in the events of that night. He would call himself 'a brand plucked from the burning', and would have understood Eliot's lines:

We only live, only suspire
Consumed by either fire or fire.

John Wesley needed desperately to be loved and to be assured of love, and was, therefore, very susceptible to female society and influence. His very close relationship to his mother is obviously germaine. As a grown man, far from home, he would crave for the Thursday nights, which as part of her regime she had devoted especially to his instruction and counselling. It would be crude and trite to say that he was 'highly-sexed'. His animal instincts always

11

remained under strict control, though he knew temptation and the intermittent misgiving and despair of the man who longs for the security of love. He was impressionable in every way, tremendously interested in the world around him, especially in the world of ideas. He was a born teacher, who must always impart to others what he had discovered himself. His friendships with women had a strong and exciting intellectual element and the would-be lover was always eager to be instructor too. Withal, he was a man of reason and logic, naturally suspicious of enthusiasm, mysticism and sentimentalism, who, like the Puritans, found that meditation was as his native air.

In his Oxford years there was a tension between his natural desire to marry one or other of the charming, cultivated girls in whose society he moved, and his longing for the 'devout and holy life' of which he read in the books to which they seem to have directed him, and which demanded celibacy as the road to perfection in a priest of the Church. He decided, encouraged by his father, to take orders and at the same time he came across the medieval Thomas à Kempis's *The Imitation of Christ*. He encountered Jeremy Taylor, the seventeenth-century bishop's *Rules and Exercises of Holy Living and Dying* with its teaching about 'purity of intention'. 'Instantly I resolved to dedicate *all my life* to God, *all* my thoughts and words and actions, being thoroughly convinced that there was no medium but that *every* part of my life (not some only) must either be a sacrifice to God or to myself; that is in effect, to the devil.'

These were very severe guides and there was that in John Wesley which revolted both against à Kempis's strictness and what a modern student has called Jeremy Taylor's 'pastoral cruelty'. But the severity could be found in the words of Christ himself, who asked for total renunciation, and Wesley capitulated, attracted as well as repelled by the rigours of the road to holiness. He began to keep a rule based on Taylor:

1 Begin and end every day with God: and sleep not immoderately.

2 Be diligent in your calling.

3 Employ all spare hours in religion; as able.

4 All holidays (holy days).

5 Avoid drunkards and busybodies.

6 Avoid curiosity, and all useless employments and knowledge.

7 Examine yourself every night.

8 Never on any account pass a day without setting aside at least an hour for devotion.

9 Avoid all manner of passion.

At this time also John Wesley discovered William Law's *Christian Perfection* and *A Serious Call to a Devout and Holy Life,* which was published in 1729. Perhaps the most pertinent remark ever made about the latter was a reply by John Keble, leader of the Oxford Movement in the next century, when Hurrell Froude had described it as 'a very clever book': 'it seemed to me as if you had said the Day of Judgment will be a pretty sight'.

William Law was a non-juring clergyman, who lived in voluntary celibacy, and for the last twenty-two years of his life kept house in community with two ladies at his native King's Cliffe in Northamptonshire. He was a mystic, and in his later period was much influenced by the esoteric teachings of Jacob Boehme, the German shoemaker, but at the time of his influence on Wesley he was very much an exponent of the seventeenth-century Anglican tradition, who wrote with exceptional clarity and power, and literary conventions that owed something to *The Spectator*. He was a great enemy of formal religion and of what Bonhoeffer in our time was to call 'cheap grace'. The type of modern nominal Christian whom he would have despised most would be the man who drives to Church in his Jaguar, trifles with the service, more interested in paraphenalia than in content, and then dashes off to a cocktail party or the golf course with never a thought of God, or of his deprived neighbour. For William Law the religion of Jesus Christ made inexorable demands.

> Devotion signifies a life given, or devoted, to God.
> He, therefore, is the devout man, who lives no longer to his own will, or the way of the world, but to the sole will of God; who serves God in everything, who makes all the parts of his common life parts of piety, by doing everything in the Name of God, and under such rules as are conformable to his glory.

All this reinforced Wesley's resolve to be 'an altogether Christian', 'all-devoted to God'. But Law also taught him not only to read but to study the Bible and to apply it to himself, to make it his 'frame of reference' for all the events, circumstances and decisions of his life. He also accepted Law's doctrine of Providence: 'Every man is to consider himself as a particular object of God's providence; under the same care and protection of God as if the world had been made for him alone. It is not by chance that a man is born at such a time, of such parents and in such a place and condition'. And much of what Wesley wrote in after years

14

about charity and the 'Catholic spirit' may be paralleled in William Law.

> There is therefore a catholic spirit, a communion of saints in the love of God and all goodness, which no-one can learn from what is called orthodoxy in particular churches, but is only to be had by a total dying to all worldly views, by a pure love of God and by such unction from above, as delivers the mind from all selfishness and makes it love truth and goodness with an equality of affection in every man, whether he be Christian, Jew, or Gentile . . .
>
> We must enter into a Catholic affection for all men, love the spirit of the Gospel wherever we see it, not work ourselves up into an abhorrence of a George Fox, or an Ignatius Loyola, but be equally glad of the light of the Gospel wherever it shines . . .

In this mood and under these influences Wesley returned to Oxford in 1729 after a brief spell as his father's curate, and immediately joined himself to the group, nicknamed 'Methodists', or the 'Holy Club', which his younger brother Charles, had helped to found. The sequel is best told in his own words of eight years later:

> In 1730 I began visiting the prisons; assisting the poor and sick in town: and doing what other good I could, by my presence or my little fortune to the bodies and souls of all men. To this end I abridged myself of all superfluities, and many that are called necessities of life. I soon became a by-word for so doing, and I rejoiced that my name was cast out as evil. The next spring I began observing the Wednesday and Friday fasts, commonly

15

observed in the ancient church; tasting no food till three in the afternoon. And now I knew not how to go any further. I diligently strove against all sin. I omitted no sort of self-denial which I thought lawful; I carefully used, both in public and private, all the means of grace at all opportunities. I omitted no occasion of doing good; I for that reason suffered evil. And all this I knew to be nothing, unless as it was directed toward inward holiness. Accordingly this, the image of God, was what I aimed at in all, by doing his will, not my own. Yet when, after continuing some years in this course I apprehended myself to be near death, I could not find that all this gave me any comfort or any assurance of acceptance with God.

Out of his frustration in Oxford, Wesley, with his brother and two friends, set sail in the autumn of 1735 for Georgia. He hoped that a mission to the Indians might make it easier for him to realise his ideal of holiness. The 'mission' was a fiasco but on the voyage he not only re-read the books that had so stirred him and studied the life of Gregory Lopez, the sixteenth century Spaniard, who became a recluse in Mexico and lived in a state of constant prayer, he met a company of Moravian refugees.

The Moravians are spiritual descendants of the smothered sects of the Middle Ages, of the Bohemian Brethren and John Hus, but they owed their eighteenth century importance to the leadership of their benefactor, Count Zinzendorf, who received them as immigrants on one of his estates in Saxony, known as Herrnhut, from whence they established themselves both in America and England. Liturgy was central to their Church life, the expression of their creed, but Zinzendorf imparted a warm, strongly evangelical tenderness, not unlike Catholic devotion to the wounds and sacred heart of Jesus.

Wesley felt that the Moravians on board ship had a secure faith and a freedom from fear, which despite all his devotion had been denied to him. They sang through the storms. The day after he landed in America he met their Bishop, Spangenberg, who asked him directly if he had 'the witness of the Spirit' as described in Romans 8 verse 16f., and also 'Do you know Jesus Christ?' Wesley replied, 'I know he is the Saviour of the world'; but Spangenberg pressed him: 'True, but do you know he has saved you?' Wesley could merely say: 'I hope he has died to save me'.

In Georgia, Wesley turned to the mystics, though he did not know the great Carmelites (Teresa of Avila and John of the Cross). But the medieval Tauler and the french Antoinette Bourignon and Molinos's *Spiritual Guide,* though they dealt so much with the indwelling Christ, did not satisfy him. To put it oversimply they offered the immediacy of communion with God which he was seeking at the price of a solitary, introspective religion, which Wesley knew was dangerous for his sociable nature, and which tended both to demean the Sacraments and to derogate the second commandment.

The mystics were countered by the study of the Fathers, the Churchmanship of Cyprian, Ephrem Syrus, defender of the Nicene faith, and Macarius 'the Egyptian'. The last-named was in fact a Syrian monk whose spirituality was derived from Gregory of Nyssa, the fourth-century Cappadocian Father, so honoured in the Eastern Orthodox Church. Yet Wesley returned to England in a state of despair. The love of woman constantly eluded him; so did the love of God.

Back in London, he met a Moravian, Peter Böhler, who made him feel that he was still 'unconverted' and ignorant of the Saviour. He was preaching with a renewed power in spite of his uncertainties and already giving offence to some of the staid, formal Church people. He himself wondered whether he should continue through lack of faith. But Böhler counselled him wisely in words that have become famous: 'Preach faith *till* you have it; and then *because* you have it you *will* preach faith'.

It was a few months after his return that, in May 1738, he went one evening 'very unwillingly' to the meeting of a religious society in Aldersgate Street, and as someone was reading from Luther's preface to the Epistle to the Romans felt his heart 'strangely warmed' and received something of the assurance of salvation for which he had been seeking.

He quarrelled with William Law whom he charged with a Pharisaic doctrine of works and failure to understand that we are saved by God's initiative not our own wearisome efforts. It is doubtful if Wesley in his evangelical ardour was quite fair to Law, but at this stage he was almost a Moravian. Almost – but not quite. His assurance was not attended by the rapturous excitement he expected. He was never as certain as Spangenberg or Böhler expected him to be, and although in August 1738 he visited Herrnhut and was impressed, he began to have reservations which increased in the following years: 'Do you not wholly neglect joint fasting? Is not the Count all in all? Do you not magnify your own Church too much?'

Those questions belong to a letter which Wesley never sent. But in 1741 he broke with the Moravians for reasons not dissimilar from those which made him suspicious of mysticism. They discountenanced the sacraments and good works. They also 'greatly checked' joy in the Holy Spirit by being so suspicious of 'animal joy', 'natural love of one another' and 'selfish love of God.'

By then, Wesley had become a field preacher. With much

hesitation, he had 'submitted to be more vile', like David dancing before the ark of the covenant, and had begun to preach in the open air. The effect was sensational. He never deserted a certain Anglican and Oxford restraint, and though he spoke with fervour and conviction, he did not descend to the tricks of the demagogue, or the cruder outbursts of the revivalist. Yet the common people hung on his words and, in the early days especially, found release from guilt and fear as they passed through paroxysms, which reminded Wesley of some of the scenes from the Gospels.

For the next fifty years he would be so occupied in turning the new industrial masses from sin to righteousness, and in helping them along the way of his own spiritual pilgrimage that he would be too busy to know whether he had a soul. He was never to experience happy marriage or a settled home. When he did marry at the age of forty-eight on the rebound from the destruction of his truest love, he turned to a wealthy widow who could not tolerate his missionary preoccupations, used him ill, and left him three times, lastly never to return.

He rode tirelessly throughout the British Isles, 225,000 miles in all, preached 40,000 sermons, changed people's lives, taught them to sing hymns, mostly the work of his brother, Charles, and organised them into societies somewhat on the Moravian model, though with Anglican and French Catholic precedents too. These, in turn, were divided into classes and bands, that, learning together and helping one another, they might grow into mature Christian life. The old Oxford name of 'Methodist' was applied to the new phenomenon, and as Ronald Knox wrote, Wesley's 'ideal did not fall short of persuading 70,000 people to adopt for all practical purposes the rules of the Holy Club'. These Methodists were as much an anxiety to him as the Corinthians and others were to St Paul. But he found his fulfilment as he lost himself in their care.

Wesley's Spirituality

The chief characteristic of Wesley's 'practical divinity' is what he would have called 'the catholic spirit' where the word 'catholic' is defined as in the passage from William Law quoted above. It has a meaning not very different from the Russian Orthodox 'Sobornost', 'we belong to one another', and comprehends many periods and traditions. Wherever there were hearts filled with the love of God in Christ, Wesley found his spiritual kinsmen. In 1741, he published *An Extract of the Life of M. de Renty, late nobleman of France*. De Renty combined mysticism with philanthropy in a remarkable way. Wesley admired his detachment from worldly (including marital) concerns as well as his devotion to Christ and the Trinity, his care for the sick, the aged and the exiles, and his formation of groups not unlike Methodist class meetings.

Between 1749 and 1755, Wesley issued his *Christian Library* in fifty volumes. This contains abridgements of Apostolic Fathers, English Puritans (in large measure), and High Churchmen, Cambridge Platonists, Scots such as Scougal, Leighton and Rutherford, Pascal, Fénélon, Molinos and the aforementioned Mexican hermit, Gregory Lopez.

The omissions are important: no medieval mystics, no Carmelites, no great reformers, no St Anthony, St Augustine, St Anselm, St Bernard, St Thomas (except indirectly through the Puritans); no one indeed whom the Catholic Church has canonised. This was due to a combination of ignorance, the unscholarly haste with which the itinerant Wesley had to read and write, and perhaps to the

20

prejudices of an age, which rather like the 1960s, was inclined to think the latest radicals wiser than the doctors of the past. But it may have bequeathed to Methodist theology a certain lack of discrimination.

But Wesley was under no doubts as to where the Christian life begins. It begins in the Divine initiative. 'We love because he first loved us.' The Gospel would not be good news if it were a summons to our search for God, to moral effort, or techniques of piety. It is the offer of the love of God in Christ, which knows no respect of persons and is free for all who will accept it, however sinful they may be.

This, if we must have labels, makes Wesley a Protestant evangelical, though Arminian, not Calvinist, that is, one who believed that grace was not irresistible and man was at liberty to reject God's offer. But he was more Catholic than Protestant in that, as Gordon Rupp has said, his spiritual theology was 'based on "love of God" rather than the "faith in Christ" of Continental and Puritan Protestantism'.

And there is a *double entendre* in the genitive. Primarily 'love of God' means, as Dom John Chapman rather brusquely wrote, 'God's, not ours, which is not worth considering'. Yet love always wants to create the response of love in the beloved. And if we are to love God in return, we must keep his law, which is to love him with our whole being, and our neighbour as ourselves. John Welsey translated a hymn of Paul Gerhardt's, the Lutheran revered in our own time by Dietrich Bonhoeffer,

Too much to thee I cannot give;
Too much I cannot do for thee;
Let all thy love and all thy grief,
Graven on my heart forever be.

This meant a disciplined, a 'methodist' life.

Wesley was even more interested in what happened after conversion to Christ than in conversion itself. The convert is but a baby in Christ and he must not be left without nurture, or given a perpetual diet of milk, or worse still, to quote Wesley, 'cordials', when he needs meat. He must be encouraged to attain nothing less than the measure of the stature of the fullness of Christ.

Wesley took with an almost dangerous seriousness the command, or what modern commentators call the 'future imperative', 'You shall be perfect as your father in heaven is perfect'. We may be critical of his teaching at this point, may think that it could foster a dangerous arrogance, and that it rested on an inadequate understanding of sin. There are times when Wesley speaks as though sin could be extracted from the personality like a rotten tooth, root and all, whereas it is part of our very being and our involvement 'in all mankind' our membership of the human race. But Wesley was clear that this perfection is perfect love, which is itself God's gift through our co-operation with his mercy. And as 'Macarius' wrote, 'it is only gradually that a man grows and comes to a *perfect man, to the measure of the stature,* not, as some would say, "Off with one coat and on with another" '.

The nerve of the doctrine is that the Christian must never be complacent about his progress in grace, his behaviour and attitudes, must not willingly go on in the same faults, the horizons of his life circumscribed by old habits, failure and ignorance. He must set no limits to the victory of the Divine love in him.

We cannot attain to perfection alone. 'The Bible knows nothing of solitary religion'. 'There is no holiness but social holiness'. In spite of his admiration for the eccentric Lopez, Wesley considered him 'much misguided' because he lived in solitide. Methodists must meet together in small groups, confess their sins to one another, relate the conflicts and the triumphs of grace and encourage one another along the royal road of universal love. He himself was genial and relaxed in the right company. Dr. Johnson said, 'John Wesley's conversation is good but he is never at leisure. He is always obliged to go at a certain hour. This is very disagreeable to a man who loves to fold his legs and have his talk out as I do'. Wesley had little in common with agricultural labourers (Methodism's success with them was later and non-Wesleyan, as they became industrially organised), and no time for aristocrats. But he liked to be with serious, intelligent, cheerful people, interested in God and the world and believed that such companionship was a means of grace.

It is because of its societary aspect as well as its pre-eminence as a sign of God's free grace that the Sacrament of Holy Communion was, for him, supreme. At a time when Church of England bishops were exhorting their clergy to interpose one celebration between Pentecost and Christmas, Wesley was receiving communion every few days. *Hymns on the Lord's Supper,* mostly the work of Charles Wesley, but with the imprint of both brothers, was published in 1745. It is a paraphrase of *The Christian Sacrament and Sacrifice* of Daniel Brevint, Dean of Lincoln, who during the Commonwealth had been a chaplain in the household of the great French Marshal Turenne. There is a high doctrine of Eucharistic sacrifice and an affirmation of the real presence, though with an agnosticism as to its manner, typical of Anglican divines such as Ruhard Hooker, who felt that transubstantiation insufficiently respected the Divine mysteries.

Austere as he was in some aspects and severe as his teaching can be, the end of Wesley's spirituality was 'joy and peace in believing'. 'Holiness is happiness' was a

23

frequent declaration. And it was because of this belief that Wesley was so censorious of the somewhat second class mystics whom he knew, calling them the most dangerous of Christianity's enemies, 'the one great anti-Christ'. He felt, rightly or wrongly, that they cultivated a state of introspective morbidity, whereas the Christian must exult in God's love, share it with his friends, and serve his neighbours, thus transcending too much anxiety over his spiritual condition, the presence or absence of God in the soul. His views were too much coloured by his own experience in the late 1730s. Later, he tempered some of his criticisms and from 1765, deleted the words about 'anti-Christ' from all editions of his Journal. He was, after all, prepared to include some mystic writers in the *Christian Library* and taught his people to sing translations of Gerhardt and Tersteegen, while there are signs that he learned from his great helper, John Fletcher of Madeley, to evaluate the mystics more justly by distinguishing between false mysticism and true, the latter Scriptural, and furthering 'the deep mysteries of inward religion' with which he himself was much concerned. As late as 1771, he wrote:

A continual desire is a continual prayer – that is, in a low sense of the word; for there is for higher sense such an open intercourse with God, such a close uninterrupted communion with Him, as Gregory Lopez experienced, and not a few of our brethren and sisters now alive.

But he could never understand why one of his preachers, John Haime, after three years of conscious communion with God, passed through a period of despair which lasted for twenty. He expected his people to enjoy their religion, and the exercises in meditation he taught them from Bishop Hall and Richard Baxter would sometimes bring them to an 'ecstatic pause' as they glimpsed something of the glories of the Kingdom of God. Special insights and graces apart they would help towards the goal, longed for in Charles Wesley's lines:

> O that my every breath were praise!
> O that my heart were filled with God!

'Our hymns', as Wesley called them, were at once the expression and the inspiration of joy, as they were of community. Wesley's rules for singing, his injunctions to sing modestly, unitedly and spiritually, are very much of the spirit of Bonhoeffer's paragraphs on 'Singing the new song', in *Life Together*. He would surely have approved of the Lutheran's words:

> The heart sings because it is overflowing with Christ
> .... all singing together that what is right must serve
> to widen our spiritual horizon, make us see our little
> company as a member of the great Christian Church on
> earth, and help us willingly or gladly to join our singing,
> be it feeble or good, to the song of the Church.

Last Years

John Wesley lived to be almost eighty-eight. He who had been stoned as a fanatic and maligned as a covert papist became revered as a national figure.

He was a reluctant founder of a new religious denomination and said that the day Methodism left the Church of England, God would leave Methodism. Yet his own irregular actions had contributed to the separation which took place less than five years after his death. Methodism had reached North America, and after the War of Independence, the members there wanted the Sacraments from their own preachers. The Bishop of London refused to help and so Wesley, who years before, had convinced himself that a presbyter had this right equally with a bishop, ordained two of his preachers and 'set apart' a third, Dr Thomas Coke, who was already a clergyman, to be 'Superintendent of the Societies in America'. Apart from this, which seems to have aroused little indignation at the time, the Church of England could hardly be expected to contain the large new order of Methodists, with their own rules, and, from 1784, legal constitution, and their ambivalent relationship to the Parish Churches. Even so, it was the Methodists who gently seceded with many protestations of loyalty and love, not the Church which drove them out, although many clergymen throughout the years had treated them with hostility and contempt and sometimes barred them from the Lord's Table.

Yet Wesley has some claim to be regarded as the greatest of all Anglican priests with his soundly orthodox theology, his comprehensive spirituality and his rare genius for evangelising the peoples of the new world – both industrialised England, and, through his preachers, North America. He, who owed so much to his natural mother, cannot be understood apart from his spiritual mother, whom he might have addressed as did one of her later sons, also an apostle of holiness, John Henry Newman: 'O my mother, whence is this unto thee, that thou hast good things poured upon thee and canst not keep them, and bearest children and darest not own them? Why hast thou not the skill to use their services, nor the heart to rejoice in their love?'

Wesley's deathbed was surrounded by his admiring disciples, according to late eighteenth-century evangelical custom. Shortly before the end, he sang one of his brother's hymns on the Incarnation, 'All glory to God in the sky!', and then Isaac Watts' paraphrase:

I'll praise my Maker while I've breath,
And when my voice is lost in death
Praise shall employ my nobler powers.

His last words, surely echoing the name, Immanuel, of the incarnate Christ, were 'The best of all is, God is with us'. And less than a week before, he had written to William Wilberforce, supporting him in his fight against the slave trade.

*

Wesley was a prodigious writer, publisher, translator. His sermons contain his standard doctrine, and, as published, many of them are more like homiletic essays than the effusions of a field preacher, though there are passages of great eloquence and passion, as well as of admirable lucidity. He engaged in numerous controversies, for he had to defend himself and his Methodists on many fronts. He was a formidable debater, who spoke, as he would say, 'plain and home' to his opponents, though always with a gospel magnanimity. He also published his journal during his own lifetime as an *apologia pro vita sua*. Many of his works were educational and on non-religious subjects, such as *Primitive Physick* and *An English Dictionary*. He was an indefatigible editor and an unashamed plagiarist, so that his devotional writings in particular and his very first book *A Collection of Forms of Prayer for Every Day of the Week* (1733) owe much to unacknowledged appropriations particularly from non-jurors. But perhaps we may recall T. S. Eliot's dictum 'lesser poets borrow, great poets steal'. Wesley's spirituality as a whole was excitingly his own.

PART TWO

From the writings of John Wesley

SOURCES

The Journal of the Revd John Wesley A.M. ed. Nehemiah Curnock (London 1938) 8 volumes

The Letters of the Revd John Wesley, A.M. ed. John Telford (London 1931) 8 volumes

The Works of the Revd John Wesley, A.M. ed. Thomas Jackson (London 1829-31) 14 volumes.

Hymns on the Lord's Supper, John and Charles Wesley reprinted in *The Eucharistic Hymns of John and Charles Wesley,* J. Ernest Rattenbury (London 1948)

The Poetical Works of John and Charles Wesley, collected and arranged by G. Osborn, D. D. (London 1868-72)

1. THE CHRISTIAN WAY

Gratitude For Our Conversion
Thee will I love, my strength, my tower;
   Thee will I love, my joy, my crown;
Thee will I love with all my power,
   In all my works and Thee alone!
Thee will I love, till the pure fire
Fill my whole soul with chaste desire.

Ah! why did I so late Thee know,
   Thee, lovelier than the sons of men!
Ah! why did I no sooner go
   To Thee, the only ease in pain!
Ashamed I sigh, and inly mourn
That I so late to Thee did turn.

In darkness willingly I stray'd;
   I sought Thee, yet from Thee I roved:
Far wide my wandering thoughts were spread,
   Thy creatures more than Thee I loved.
And now, if more at length I see,
   'Tis through Thy light, and comes from Thee.

I thank Thee, Uncreated Sun,
   That Thy bright beams on me have shined;
I thank Thee, who hast overthrown

My foes, and heal'd my wounded mind;
I thank Thee, whose enlivening voice
Bids my freed heart in Thee rejoice.

Give to my eyes refreshing tears;
    Give to my heart, chaste, hallow'd fires;
Give to my soul, with filial fears,
    The love that all heaven's host inspires:
'That all my powers with all their might
In Thy sole glory may unite.'

Thee will I love, my joy, my crown!
    Thee will I love, my Lord, my God!
Thee will I love, beneath Thy frown
    Or smile, Thy sceptre or Thy rod.
What though my flesh and heart decay?
Thee shall I love in endless day!

From the German of Johann Angelus Scheffler
Poetical Works, Vol. 1. pp 176-7

To abandon all, to strip one's self of all, in order to seek
and to follow Jesus Christ naked to Bethlehem, where He
was born; naked to the hall where He was scourged; and
naked to Calvary, where He died on the Cross, is so great a
mercy, that neither the thing, nor the knowledge of it, is
given to any, but through faith in the Son of God.

Works Vol. XI p.435

Q What was the rise of Methodism, so called?
A In 1729, two young men, reading the Bible, saw they
could not be saved without holiness, followed after it, and
incited others to do so. In 1737, they saw holiness comes by

faith. They saw likewise that men are justified before they are sanctified; but still holiness was their point. God then thrust them out, utterly against their will, to raise a holy people.

Works, Vol. VIII, p. 300 Minutes of the first Annual Conference.

I was early warned against laying, as the papists do, too much stress on outward works – or on a faith without works; which, as it does not include, so it will never lead to, true hope or charity. . . . but before God's time was come, I fell among some Lutheran and Calvinist authors, whose confused and indigested accounts magnified faith to such an amazing size that it quite hid the rest of the commandments. I did not see then that this was the natural effect of their overgrown fear of popery, being so terrified with the cry of merit and good works that they plunged at once into the other extreme. In this labyrinth I was utterly lost, not being able to find out what the error was, nor yet to reconcile this uncouth hypothesis either with Scripture or common sense.

The English writers, such as Bishop Beveridge, Bishop Taylor and Mr Nelson, a little relieved me from these well-meaning, wrong-headed Germans. Their accounts of Christianity I could easily see to be, in the main, consistent both with reason and Scripture. Only when they interpreted Scripture in different ways I was often much at a loss. And again, there was one thing much insisted on in Scripture – the unity of the Church – which none of them, I thought, clearly explained or strongly inculcated.

Journal Sun 8 January 1738

Q What is faith?

A Faith, in general, is a divine supernatural evidence or manifestation of things not seen, i.e. of past, future, or spiritual things. 'Tis a spiritual sight of God and the things of God. Therefore repentance is a low species of faith, i.e. a supernatural sense of an offended God. Justifying faith is a supernatural inward sense or sight of God in Christ reconciling the world unto himself. First, a sinner is convinced by the Holy Ghost: "Christ loved me and gave himself for me". This is that faith by which he is justified, or pardoned, the moment he receives it. Immediately the same Spirit bears witness. "Thou art pardoned, thou hast redemption in his blood". And this is saving faith, whereby the love of God is shed abroad in his heart.

Works, Vol. VIII p. 275, Minutes of the first Annual Conference, June 25th, 1744

If you allow that it is reasonable to love God, to love mankind and to do good to all men, you cannot but allow that religion which we preach and live to be agreeable to the highest reason.

Perhaps this is all you can bear. It is tolerable enough, and if we spoke only of being 'saved by love' you should have no great objection: but you do not comprehend what we say of being 'saved by *faith*'. I know you do not. You do not in any degree comprehend what we mean by that expression. Have patience, then, and I will tell you yet again. By those words 'we are saved by faith', we mean that the moment a man receives that faith which is above described he is saved from doubt and sorrow of heart, by a peace that passes all understanding; from the heaviness of a wounded spirit by joy unspeakable; and from his sins, of whatever kind they were, from vicious desires, as well as words and actions, by the love of God and of all mankind then shed abroad in his heart.

An Earnest Appeal to Men of Reason and Religion
1743, paras. 22 and 23.

Should it still be inquired, 'How does the Spirit of God "bear witness with our spirit, that we are the children of God," so as to exclude all doubt, and evince the reality of our sonship?' – the answer is clear from what has been observed above. And first, as to the witness of our spirit: the soul as intimately and evidently perceives when it loves, delights, and rejoices in God, as when it loves and delights in anything on earth. And it can no more doubt, whether it loves, delights, and rejoices or no, than whether it exists or no. If, therefore, this be just reasoning.'

He that now loves God, that delights and rejoices in Him with an humble joy, an holy delight, and an obedient love, is a child of God:

But I thus love, delight, and rejoice in God;

Therefore, I am a child of God.

Then a Christian can in no wise doubts of his being a child of God. Of the former proposition he has as full an assurance as he has that the Scriptures are of God; and of his thus loving God, he has an inward proof, which is nothing short of self-evidence. Thus, the testimony of our own spirit is with the most intimate conviction manifested to our hearts, in such a manner, as beyond all reasonable doubt to evince the reality of our sonship.

Sermons, Vol. 1, p. 209f.

Some are fond of the expression (assurances): I am not; I

hardly ever use it. But I will simply declare (having neither leisure nor inclination to draw the saw of controversy concerning it) what are my present sentiments with regard to the thing which is usually meant thereby.

I believe a few, but very few, Christians have an assurance from God of everlasting salvation; and that is the thing which the Apostle terms the plerophory or full assurance of hope.

I believe more have such an assurance of being now in the favour of God as excludes all doubt and fear. And this, if I do not mistake, the Apostle means by the plerophory or full assurance of faith.

I believe a consciousness of being in the favour of God (which I do not term plerophory, or full assurance, since it is frequently weakened, nay, perhaps interrupted, by returns of doubt or fear) is the common privilege of Christians, fearing God and working righteousness.

Yet I do not affirm there are no exceptions to this general rule. Possibly some may be in the favour of God, and yet go mourning all the day long. But I believe this is usually owing either to disorder of body or ignorance of the gospel promises.

Therefore I have not for many years thought a consciousness of acceptance to be essential to justifying faith.

And after I have thus explained myself once for all, I think without any evasion or ambiguity, I am sure without any self-contradiction, I hope all reasonable men will be satisfied. And whoever will still dispute with me on this head must do it for disputing's sake.

Works, Vol. XIV, pp. 360-1

There is no love of God without patience, and no patience without lowliness and sweetness of spirit.

Humility and patience are the surest proofs of the increase of love.

Humility alone unites patience with love; without which it is impossible to draw profit from suffering; or indeed, to avoid complaint, especially when we think we have given no occasion for what men make us suffer.

Works Vol. XI, p.436

Expect contradiction and opposition, together with crosses of various kinds. Consider the words of St. Paul: 'To you it is given, in the behalf of Christ' – for His sake, as a fruit of His death and intercession for you – 'not only to believe, but also to suffer from His sake' (*Phil.* i. 29). *It is given!* God gives you this opposition or reproach; it is a fresh token of His love. And will you disown the Giver; or spurn His gift, and count it a misfortune? Will you not rather say, 'Father, the hour is come, that Thou shouldest be glorified: Now Thou givest Thy child to suffer something for Thee: Do with me according to Thy will?' Know that these things, far from being hinderances to the work of God, or to your soul, unless by your own fault, are not only unavoidable in the course of Providence, but profitable, yea, necessary, for you. Therefore, receive them from God (not from chance) with willingness, with thankfulness. Receive them from men with humility, meekness, yieldingness, gentleness, sweetness.

Works, Vol. XI, p. 433; First published 1762;
re-issued in *A Plain Account of Christian Perfection* 1777

The perfection I hold is so far from being contrary to the doctrine of our Church, that it is exactly the same which every Clergyman prays for every Sunday: "Cleanse the thoughts of our hearts by the inspiration of thy Holy Spirit, that we may perfectly love thee, and worthily magnify thy holy name". I mean neither more nor less than this.

Works, Vol. X, 450

The 'gospel preachers' so called corrupt their hearers; they vitiate their taste, so that they cannot relish sound doctrine; and spoil their appetite, so that they cannot turn it into nourishment; they, as it were, feed them with sweetmeats, till the genuine wine of the kingdom seems quite insipid to them. They give them cordial upon cordial, which make them all life and spirit for the present; but meantime their appetite is destroyed, so that they can neither retain nor digest the pure milk of the Word.

This was the very case when I went last into the North. For some time before my coming John Downes had scarce been able to preach at *all:* the three others in the Round were such as styled themselves 'gospel preachers'. When I came to review the Societies, with great expectation of finding a vast increase, I found most of them lessened by one third; one entirely broken up; that of Newcastle itself was less by a hundred members than when I visited it before; and of those that remained, the far greater number in every place were cold, weary, heartless, and dead. Such were the blessed effects of this *gospel-preaching,* of this *new* method of *preaching Christ!*

On the other hand, when in my return I took an account of the Societies in Yorkshire, chiefly under the care of John Nelson, one of the *old* way, in whose preaching you could find no life, no food, I found them all alive, strong, and vigorous of soul, believing, loving, praising God their Saviour, and increased in number from eighteen or nineteen hundred to upwards of three thousand. These had been continually fed with that wholesome food which *you* could neither relish nor digest. From the beginning they had been taught both the law and the gospel. 'God loves *you:* therefore love and obey him. Christ died for *you:* therefore die to sin. Christ is risen: therefore rise in the image of God. Christ liveth evermore: therefore live to God, till you live with Him in glory.'

So *we* preached; and so you believed. This is the scriptural way, the *Methodist* way, the true way. God grant we may never turn therefrom, to the right hand or to the left.

Letters, Vol. III, pp. 81-5

God is the first object of our love: Its next office is, to bear the defects of others. And we should begin the practice of this amidst our own household.

We should chiefly exercise our love towards them who most shock either our way of thinking, or our temper, or our knowledge, or the desire we have that others should be as virtuous as we wish to be ourselves.

Works, Vol. XL, p. 438

2. RULE OF LIFE

Likewise, if you would avoid schism, observe every rule of the Society, and of the Bands, for conscience' sake. Never omit meeting your Class or Band; never absent yourself from any public meeting. These are the very sinews of our Society; and whatever weakens, or tends to weaken, our regard for these, or our exactness in attending them, strikes at the very root of our community. As one saith, 'That part of our economy, the private weekly meetings for prayer, examination, and particular exhortation, has been the greatest means of deepening and confirming every blessing that was received by the word preached, and of diffusing it to others, who could not attend the public ministry; whereas, without this religious connection and intercourse, the most ardent attempts, by mere preaching, have proved of no lasting use.'

Works Vol. XI, p.433

First published 1762: re-issued in *A Plain Account of Christian Perfection* 1777

Rules of the Band Societies

The design of our meeting is, to obey that command of God, 'Confess your faults one to another, and pray for one another, that ye may be healed.'

To this end, we intend,–

1. To meet once a week, at the least.

2. To come punctually at the hour appointed, without some extraordinary reason.

3. To begin (those of us who are present) exactly at the hour, with singing or prayer.

4. To speak each of us in order, freely and plainly, the true state of our souls, with the faults we have committed in thought, word, or deed, and the temptations we have felt, since our last meeting.

5. To end every meeting with prayer, suited to the state of each person present.

6. To desire some person among us to speak his own state first, and then to ask the rest, in order, as many and as searching questions as may be, concerning their state, sins, and temptations.

Some of the questions proposed to every one before he is admitted among us may be to this effect:

1. Have you the forgiveness of your sins?

2. Have you peace with God, through our Lord Jesus Christ?

3. Have you the witness of God's Spirit with your spirit, that you are a child of God?

4. Is the love of God shed abroad in your heart?

5. Has no sin, inward or outward, dominion over you?

6. Do you desire to be told of your faults?

7. Do you desire to be told of all your faults, and that plain and home?

8. Do you desire that every one of us should tell you, from time to time, whatsoever is in his heart concerning you?

9. Consider! Do you desire we should tell you whatsoever we think, whatsoever we fear, whatsoever we hear, concerning you?

10. Do you desire that, in doing this, we should come as close as possible, that we should cut to the quick, and search your heart to the bottom?

11. Is it your desire and design to be on this, and all other occasions, entirely open, so as to speak everything that is in your heart without exception, without disguise, and without reserve?

Any of the preceding questions may be asked as often as occasion offers; the four following at every meeting:

1. What known sins have you committed since our last meeting?

2. What temptations have you met with?

3. How were you delivered?

4. What have you thought, said, or done, of which you doubt whether it be sin or not?

Drawn up December 25, 1738

Works, Vol. VIII, pp. 272-3

Directions Given to the Band Societies

You are supposed to have the faith that 'overcometh the world.'

To you, therefore, it is not grievous—

I. Carefully to abstain from doing evil; in particular—

1. Neither to buy nor sell anything at all on the Lord's day.

2. To taste no spirituous liquor, no dram of any kind, unless prescribed by a Physician.

3. To be at a word in buying and selling.

4. To pawn nothing, no, not to save life.

5. Not to mention the fault of any behind his back, and to stop those short that do.

6. To wear no needless ornaments, such as rings, earrings, necklaces, lace, ruffles.

7. To use no needless self-indulgence, such as taking snuff or tobacco, unless prescribed by a Physician.

II. Zealously to maintain good works; in particular—

1. To give alms of such things as you possess, and that to the uttermost of your power.

2. To reprove all that sin in your sight, and that in love and meekness of wisdom.

3. To be patterns of diligence and frugality, of self-denial, and taking up the cross daily.

III. Constantly to attend on all the ordinances of God; in particular—

1. To be at church and at the Lord's table every week, and at every public meeting of the Bands.

2. To attend the ministry of the word every morning, unless distance, business, or sickness prevent.

3. To use private prayer every day; and family prayer, if you are at the head of a family.

4. To read the Scriptures, and meditate therein, at every vacant hour. And,—

5. To observe, as days of fasting or abstinence, all Fridays in the year.

December 25, 1744
Works, Vol. VIII, pp. 273-4

If then a doubt should at any time arise in your mind concerning what you are going to expend, either on yourself or any part of your family, you have an easy way to remove it. Calmly and seriously inquire:

1. In expending this, am I acting according to my character? Am I acting herein, not as a proprietor, but as a steward of my Lord's goods?

2. Am I doing this in obedience to his Word? In what Scripture does he require me so to do?

3. Can I offer up this action, this expense, as a sacrifice to God through Jesus Christ?

4. Have I reason to believe that for this very work I shall have a reward at the resurrection of the just?

*

... You see the nature and extent of truly Christian prudence so far as it relates to the use of that great talent, money. *Gain all you can,* without hurting either yourself or your neighbour, in soul or body, by applying hereto with unintermitted diligence and with all the understanding which God has given you. *Save all you can,* by cutting off every expense which serves only to indulge foolish desire, to gratify either the desire of the flesh, the desire of the eye, or the pride of life (cf. 1Jn. 2:16). Waste nothing, living or dying on sin or folly, whether for yourself or your children. And then *give all you can;* or, in other words, give all you have to God.

The Use of Money, Sermons, Vol. II, 309-27

A Scheme of Self-Examination Used by the First Methodists in Oxford
Sunday. LOVE OF GOD AND SIMPLICITY: means of which are Prayer and Meditation.
1. Have I been simple and recollected in everything I said or did? Have I a) been *simple* in everything, i.e. looked upon God, my Good, my Pattern, my One Desire, my Disposer, Parent of Good; acted wholly for Him; bounded my Views with the present action or hour? b) *Recollected?* i.e. Has this simple view been distinct and uninterrupted? Have I, in order to keep it so, used the signs agreed upon with my

Friends wherever I was? Have I done anything without a previous perception of its being the Will of God! Or, without a perception of its being an Exercise or a Means of the Virtue of the day? Have I said anything without it?

2. Have I prayed with fervor? At going in and out of Church? In the Church? Morning and evening in private? Monday, Wednesday, and Friday, with my Friends, at rising? Before lying down? On Saturday noon? All the time I am engaged in exterior work in private? Before I go into the place of public or private prayer, for help therein? Have I wherever I was, gone to Church morning and evening, unless for necessary mercy? And spent from one hour to three in private? Have I in private prayer frequently stopt short and observed what fervor? Have I repeated it over and over, till I adverted to every word? Have I at the beginning of every prayer or paragraph owned I cannot pray? Have I paused before I concluded in his Name, and adverted to *my Saviour* now interceding for me at the right-hand of God, and offering up these prayers?

3. Have I duly used Ejaculations? i.e. Have I every hour prayed for Humility, Faith, Hope, Love, and the particular Virtue of the day? Considered, with *whom* I was the last hour, *what* I did and *how?* With regard to Recollection, Love of Man, Humility, Self-denial, Resignation, and Thankfulness? Considered the next hour in the same respects, offered up all I do to my Redeemer, begged his assistance in every particular, and commended my soul to his keeping? Have I done this deliberately (not in haste), seriously, (not doing any thing else the while) and fervently as I could?

4. Have I duly prayed for the Virtue of the day? i.e. Have I prayed for it at going out and coming in? Deliberately, seriously, fervently?

5. Have I used a Collect at nine, twelve, and three? And

Grace before and after eating? (aloud at my own room). Deliberately, seriously, fervently?

6. Have I duly meditated? Every day, unless for necessary mercy, a) From six etc. to prayers? b) From four to five, (What was particular in the Providence of this day?) How ought the Virtue of the day to have been exerted upon it? How did it fall short? (Here faults.) c) On Sunday from six to seven, with Kempis? From three to four on Redemption, or God's Attributes? Wednesday and Friday from twelve to one on the Passion? After ending a book, on what I had marked in it?

Reprinted by Wesley in the *Arminian Magazine*, 1781
Works, Vol. XI, pp. 514-15

Monday. Love of Man

1. Have I been zealous to do, and active in doing good? i.e. a) Have I embraced every probable opportunity of doing good, and preventing, removing, or lessening evil? b) Have I pursued it with my might? c) Have I thought anything too dear to part with, to serve my neighbour? d) Have I spent an hour at least every day in speaking to someone or other? e) Have I given anyone up, till he *expressly* renounced me? f) Have I, before I spoke to any, learned, as far as I could, his temper, way of thinking, past life, and peculiar hinderances, internal and external? Fixt the point to be aimed at? Then the means to it? g) Have I in speaking, proposed the motives, then the difficulties, then balanced them, then exhorted him to consider both calmly and deeply, and to pray earnestly for help? h) Have I, in speaking to a stranger, explained what Religion is not, (not negative, not external) and what it is, (a recovery of the image of God), searched at what step in it he stops, and what makes him stop there?

Exhorted and directed him? i) Have I persuaded all I could to attend public Prayers, Sermons and Sacraments? And in general, to obey the laws of the Church Catholic, the Church of *England,* the State, the University, and their respective Colleges? j) Have I, when taxed with any act of obedience, avowed it, and turned the attack with sweetness and firmness? k) Have I disputed upon any practical point, unless it was to be practised just then? l) Have I in disputing, (1.) Desired him, To define the terms of the question. To limit it: what he grants, what denies: (2.) Delayed speaking my opinion; let him explain and prove his: then insinuated and pressed objections? m) Have I after every visit, asked him who went with me, Did I say any thing wrong? n) Have I, when any one asked Advice, directed and exhorted him with all my power?

2. Have I rejoiced with and for my neighbour in Virtue or Pleasure? Grieved with him in pain, for him in sin?

3. Have I received his infirmities with pity, not anger?

4. Have I thought or spoke unkindly of or to him? Have I revealed any evil of any one, unless it was necessary to some *particular* good I had in view? Have I then done it with all the tenderness of phrase and manner, consistent with that end? Have I any way appeared to approve them that did otherwise?

5. Has good-will been, and appeared to be, the spring of all my actions towards others?

6. Have I duly used intercession? a) Before, b) after speaking to any? c) For my Friends on Sunday? d) For my Pupils on Monday? e) For those who have particularly desired it, on Wednesday and Friday? f) For the Family in which I am, every day?

Ibid., pp. 515-17

Love fasts when it can, and as much as it can. It leads to all the ordinances of God, and employs itself in all the outward works whereof it is capable. It flies, as it were, like Elijah over the plain, to find God upon His holy mountain.

Works, Vol. XI, p. 439

'But is it not better to abstain from pride and vanity, from foolish and hurtful desires, from peevishness, and anger, and discontent, than from food? 'Without question, it is. But here again we have to remind you of our Lord's words: 'These things ought ye to have done, and not to leave the other undone.' And indeed, the latter is only in order to the former; it is a means to that great end. We abstain from food with this view – that, by the grace of God conveyed into our souls through this outward means, in conjunction with all the other channels of His grace which He hath appointed, we may be enabled to abstain from every passion and temper which is not pleasing in His sight. We refrain from the one, that, being endued with power from on high, we may be able to refrain from the other. So that your argument proves just the contrary to what you designed. It proves that we ought to fast. For if we ought to abstain from evil tempers and desires, then we ought thus to abstain from food; since these little instances of self-denial are the ways God hath chose, wherein to bestow that great salvation.

Sermons, Vol. 1, p. 451ff.

3. THE CATHOLIC SPIRIT

But although a difference in opinions or modes of worship may prevent an entire external union, yet need it prevent our union in affection? Though we cannot think alike, may we not love alike? May we not be of one heart, though we are not of one opinion? Without all doubt, we may. Herein all the children of God may unite, not withstanding these smaller differences. These remaining as they are, they may forward one another in love and in good works.

Sermons, Vol. II, p. 126

In some of the following days I snatched a few hours to read *The History of the Puritans.* I stand in amaze: first, at the execrable spirit of persecution which drove those venerable men out of the Church, and with which Queen Elizabeth's clergy were as deeply tinctured as ever Queen Mary's were; secondly, at the weakness of those holy confessors, many of whom spent so much of their time and strength in disputing about surplices and hoods, or kneeling at the Lord's Supper.

Journal, Wed. 4 March 1747

. . . you think I ought to "sit still" because otherwise I should invade another's office if I interfered with other people's business and intermeddled with souls that did not belong to me. You accordingly ask, "How is it that I assemble Christians who are none of my charge, to sing psalms and pray and hear the Scriptures expounded?" and think it hard to justify doing this in other men's parishes upon "catholic principles".

Permit me to speak plainly. If by "catholic principles" you mean any other than scriptural, they weigh nothing with *me* . . .

Suffer me now to tell you *my* principles in this matter. I look upon *all the world as my parish* – thus far I mean, that in whatever part of it I am, I judge it meet, right and my bounden duty to declare unto all that are willing to hear me the glad tidings of salvation.

Letter to James Hervey, March 20th, 1739

Beware of schism, of making a rent in the Church of Christ. That inward disunion, the members ceasing to have a reciprocal love 'one for another' (1 *Cor.* xii, 25), is the very root of all contention, and every outward separation. Beware of everything tending thereto. Beware of a dividing spirit; shun whatever has the least aspect that way. Therefore, say not, 'I am of Paul or of Apollos'; the very thing which occasioned the schism at Corinth. Say not, 'This is my Preacher; the best Preacher in England. Give me him, and take all the rest.' All this tends to breed or foment division, to disunite those whom God hath joined. Do not despise or run down any Preacher; do not exalt any one above the rest, lest you hurt both him and the cause of God. On the other hand, do not bear hard upon any by reason of some incoherency or inaccuracy of expression; no, nor for some mistakes, were they really such.

Works, Vol. XI, p. 433

Beware of tempting others to separate from you. Give no offence which can possibly be avoided; see that your practice be in all things suitable to your profession, adorning the doctrine of God our Saviour. Be particularly careful in speaking of yourself. You may not, indeed, deny the work of God; but speak of it, when you are called thereto, in the most inoffensive manner possible. Avoid all magnificent, pompous words; indeed, you need give it no general name; neither perfection, sanctification, the second blessing, nor the having attained. Rather speak of the particulars which God has wrought for you. You may say, 'At such a time I felt a change which I am not able to express; and since that time, I have not felt pride, or self-will, or anger, or unbelief; not anything but a fulness of love to God and to all mankind.' And answer any other plain question that is asked, with modesty and simplicity.

And if any of you should at any time fall from what you now are, if you should again feel pride or unbelief, or any temper from which you are now delivered; do not deny, do not hide, do not disguise it at all, at the peril of your soul. At all events go to one in whom you can confide, and speak just what you feel. God will enable him to speak a word in season, which shall be health to your soul. And surely He will again lift up your head, and cause the bones that have been broken to rejoice.

Ibid, p. 434
First published 1762; re-issued in *A Plain Account of Christian Perfection*, 1777

Suffer not one thought of separating from your brethren, whether their opinions agree with yours or not. Do not dream that any man sins in not believing you, in not taking your word; or that this or that opinion is essential to the work, and both must stand or fall together. Beware of impatience of contradiction. Do not condemn or think hardly of those who cannot see just as you see, or who judge it their duty to contradict you, whether in a great thing or a small. I fear some of us have thought hardly of others, merely because they contradicted what we affirmed. All this tends to division; and, by everything of this kind, we are teaching them an evil less against ourselves.

O beware of touchiness, of testiness, not bearing to to be spoken to; starting at the least word; and flying from those who do not implicitly receive mine or another's sayings!

Ibid., p. 434

I administered the Lord's Supper to near two hundred communicants: so solemn a season I never remember to have known in the city of Norwich. As a considerable number of them were Dissenters, I desired every one to use what posture he judged best. Had I required them to kneel, probably half would have sat. Now all but one kneeled down.

*

I met them all at six, requiring every one to show his ticket when he came in: a thing that had never been heart of before. I likewise insisted on another strange regulation, that the men and women should sit apart. A third was made the same day. It had been a custom ever since the Tabernacle was built, to have the galleries full of spectators while the Lord's Supper was administered. This I judged highly improper; and therefore ordered none to be admitted, but those who desired to communicate. And I found far less difficulty than I expected, in bringing them to submit to this also.

Journal, July 18th and April 1st, 1759

If God still loveth us, we ought also to love one another. We ought, without this endless jangling about opinions, to provoke one another to love and to good works. Let the points whereon we differ stand aside: here are enough wherein we agree, enough to be the ground of every Christian temper and of every Christian action. . . .

In the name then, and in the strength of God, let us resolve, first, not to hurt one another; to do nothing unkind or unfriendly to each other, nothing we would not have done to ourselves. Rather let us endeavour after every instance of a kind, friendly, and Christian behaviour towards each other.

Let us resolve, secondly, God being our helper, to speak nothing harsh or unkind of each other. The sure way to avoid this is to say all the good we can both of and to one another; in all our conversation, either with or concerning each other to use only the language of love, to speak with all softness and tenderness, with the most endearing expression which is consistent with truth and sincerity.

Let us, thirdly, resolve to harbour no unkind thought, no unfriendly temper towards each other. Let us lay the axe to the root of the tree; let us examine all that rises in our heart, and suffer no disposition there which is contrary to tender affection. Then we shall easily refrain from unkind actions and words, when the very root of bitterness is cut up.

Let us, fourthly, endeavour to help each other on in whatever we are agreed leads to the kingdom. So far as we can let us always rejoice to strengthen each other's hands in God. Above all, let us each take heed to himself . . . that he fall not short of the religion of love . . .

Letters, Vol. III, pp. 12-14

4. SACRAMENT AND PRAYER

Why did my dying Lord ordain
This dear memorial of his love?
Might we not all by faith obtain,
By faith the mountain sin remove,
Enjoy the sense of sins forgiven,
And holiness, the taste of heaven?

It seem'd to my Redeemer good
That faith should *here* his coming wait,
Should here receive immortal food,
Grow up in him Divinely great,
And, filled with holy violence, seize
The glorious crown of righteousness.

Saviour, thou didst the mystery give,
That I thy nature might partake;
Thou bidd'st me outward signs receive,
One with thyself my soul to make;
My body, soul, and spirit to join
Inseparably one with thine.

The prayer, the fast, the word conveys,
When mix'd with faith, thy life to me;
In all the channels of thy grace
I still have fellowship with thee:

But chiefly here my soul is fed
With fullness of immortal bread.

John and Charles Wesley,
Hymns on the Lord's Supper, 54

With solemn faith we offer up
And spread before thy glorious eyes,
That only ground of all our hope,
That precious, bleeding sacrifice,
Which brings thy grace on sinners down,
And perfects all our souls in one.

Ibid., 125

We need not now go up to heaven,
To bring the long-sought Saviour down;
Thou art to all already given,
Thou dost even now thy banquet crown;
To every faithful soul appear,
And show thy real presence here!

Ibid., 116

All that a Christian does, even in eating and sleeping, is prayer, when it is done in simplicity, according to the order of God, without either adding to our diminishing from it by his own choice.

Prayer continues in the desire of the heart, though the understanding be employed on outward things.

In souls filled with love, the desire to please God is a continual prayer.

Works, Vol. XI, p. 435

Although all the graces of God depend on His mere bounty, yet is He pleased generally to attach them to the prayers, the instructions, and the holiness of those with whom we are. By strong though invisible attractions. He draws some souls through their intercourse with others.

Ibid., p. 435

The bottom of the soul may be in repose, even while we are in many outward troubles; just as the bottom of the sea is calm, while the surface is strongly agitated.

Ibid., p. 435

In the greatest temptations, a single look to Christ, and the barely pronouncing His name, suffices to overcome the wicked one, so it be done with confidence and calmness of spirit.

Ibid., p. 436

It is scarce conceivable how strait the way is wherein God leads them that follow Him; and how dependent on Him we must be, unless we are wanting in our faithfulness to Him.

As a very little dust will disorder a clock, and the least sand will obscure our sight, so the least grain of sin which is upon the heart will hinder its right motion towards God.

Ibid., p. 435

At many times our advances in the race that is set before us are clear and perceptible; at other times they are no more perceptible (at least to ourselves) than the growth of a tree. At any time you may pray –

Strength and comfort from thy word,
    Imperceptibly supply.

And when you perceive nothing, it does not follow that the work of God stands still in your soul; especially while your desire is unto him, and while you choose him for your portion. He does not leave you to yourself, though it may seem so to your apprehension. The difference between temptation and sin is generally plain enough to all that are simple of heart; but in some exempt cases it is not plain. There we want the unction of the Holy One. Voluntary humility, calling every defect a sin, is not well pleasing to God. Sin, properly speaking, is neither more nor less than "a voluntary transgression of a known law of God".

Works, Vol. XII, 432

It is a blessing indeed when God uncovers our hearts and clearly shows us what spirit we are of. But there is no manner of necessity that this self-knowledge should make us miserable. Certainly the highest degree of it is well consistent both with peace and joy in the Holy Ghost. Therefore how deeply soever you may be convinced of pride, self-will, peevishness, or any other inbred sin, see that you do not let go that confidence whereby you may still rejoice in God your Saviour. Some indeed, have been quite unhappy, though they retained their faith, through desire on the one hand and conviction on the other. But that is nothing to you; you need never give up anything which you have already received.

It is a great thing to spend all our time to the glory of God. But you need not be scrupulous as to the precise time of reading and praying; I mean as to the dividing it between one and the other. A few minutes one way or the other are of no great importance.

May He who loves you fill you with his pure love!

Letters, IV, 85

Whither, O my God, should we wander, if left to ourselves? Whither should we fix our hearts if not directed by Thee?

Thou didst send forth Thy Holy Spirit to guide and comfort us; and give Thyself in the Holy Eucharist to feed and nourish our hungry souls with that sacramental food.

Still Thou art really present to us in that holy mystery of love; hence we offer up our devotions in it with our utmost reverence wonder and love.

These saving mysteries keep alive our dear Redeemer's death and apply to our souls all the merits of His passion.

Blessed are the eyes, O Jesu, that see Thee in these holy signs; and blessed is the mouth that reverently receives Thee.

Blessed yet more is the heart that desires Thy coming.

Devotions for Every Day in the Week
(Thursday), based on the Roman Catholic,
John Austin, (*Christian Library,* Vol. XIII, 1755)

5. JOURNEY AND PERILS

Nearly thirty years ago, I was thinking, 'How is it that no horse ever stumbles while I am reading?' (history, poetry and philosophy I commonly read on horseback, having other employment at other times.) No account can possibly be given but this: because then I throw the reins on his neck. I then set myself to observe; and I aver, that in riding above an hundred thousand miles, I scarce ever remember any horse (except two that would fall head over heels any way) to fall, or make a considerable stumble while I rode with a slack rein. To fancy, therefore that a tight rein prevents stumbling is a capital blunder. I have repeated the trial more frequently than most men in the kingdom can do. A slack rein will prevent stumbling if anything will. But in some horses nothing can.

Journal, Wednesday March 21st, 1770

Field Preaching

In the evening I reached Bristol, and met Mr Whitefield there. I could scarce reconcile myself at first to this strange way of preaching in the fields, of which he set me an example on Sunday; having been all my life (till very lately) so tenacious of every point relating to decency and order, that

I should have thought the saving of souls almost a sin, if it had not been done in church.

Journal, Sat. March 31st 1739

In the evening (Mr Whitefield being gone) I began expounding our Lord's Sermon on the Mount (one pretty remarkable precedent of field-preaching, though I suppose there were churches at that time also), to a little society which was accustomed to meet once or twice a week in Nicholas Street.

Journal, Sun. April 1st 1739

At four in the afternoon, I submitted to be more vile, and proclaimed in the highways the glad tidings of salvation, speaking from a little eminence in a ground adjoining to the city, to about three thousand people.

Journal, Mon. April 2nd 1739

On Monday and Tuesday evening I preached abroad, near the Keelmen's Hospital, to twice the people we should have had at the house. What marvel the devil does not love field-preaching? Neither do I: I love a commodious room, a soft cushion, an handsome pulpit. But where is my zeal, if I do not trample all these under foot, in order to save one more soul?

Journal, Sat. June 9th 1759

Can you sustain them if you would? Can you bear the summer rain to beat upon your naked head? Can you suffer the wintry rain or wind, from whatever quarter it blows?

Are you able to stand in the open air without any covering or defence when God casteth abroad his snow like wool, or scattereth his hoar frost like ashes? And yet these are some of the smallest inconveniences which accompany field--preaching. For beyond all these are the contradiction of sinners, the scoffs both of the great, vulgar small; contempt and reproach of every kind; often more than verbal affronts, stupid, brutal violence, sometimes to the hazard of health, or limbs, or life, Brethren do you envy us this honour? What, I pray, would buy you to be a field preacher? Or what, think you, could induce any man of common sense to continue therein one year, unless he had a full conviction in himself that it was the will of God concerning him?

Works, Volume VIII, p. 231

There was great expectation at Bath, of what a noted man was to do to me there; and I was much entreated not to preach, because no one knew what might happen. By this report I also gained a much larger audience, among whom were many of the rich and great. I told them plainly, the Scripture had concluded them all under sin – high and low, rich and poor, one with another. Many of them seemed to be a little surprised, and were sinking apace into seriousness, when their champion appeared, and coming close to me, asked by what authority I did these things. I replied, "by the authority of Jesus Christ, conveyed to me by the (now) Archbishop of Canterbury, when he laid his hands upon me, and said, 'Take thou authority to preach the gospel!' " He said "This is contrary to Act of Parliament: this is a conventicle." I answered, "Sir, the conventicles mentioned in that Act (as the preamble shows) are seditious meetings: but this is not such; here is no shadow of sedition; therefore it is not contrary to that Act.

He replied, "I say it is: and, beside, your preaching frightens people out of their wits". "Sir, did you ever hear me preach?" "No". "How then can you judge of what you never heard?" "Sir, by common report." "Common report is not enough. Give me leave, sir, to ask, Is not your name Nash?" "My name is Nash." "Sir I dare not judge of you by common report: I think it not enough to judge by." Here he paused awhile, and, having recovered himself, said, "I desire to know what this people comes here for:" on which one replied, "Sir, leave him to me: let an old woman answer him. You, Mr Nash take care of your body; we take care of our souls; and for the food of our souls we come here." He replied not a word, but walked away.

Journal, June 5th, 1739

I rode to Wednesbury . . . Before five the mob surrounded the house again in greater numbers than ever. The cry of one and all was, "Bring out the minister; we will have the minister". I desired one to take their captain by the hand, and bring him into the house. After a few sentences interchanged between us, the lion was become a lamb. I desired him to go and bring one or two more of the most angry of his companions. He brought in two, who were ready to swallow the ground with rage; but in two minutes they were as calm as he. I then bade them make way, that I might go out among the people. As soon as I was in the midst of them, I called for a chair; and, standing up, asked, "What do any of you want with me?" Some said, "We want you to go with us to the justice." I replied, "That I will, with all my heart".

(The justices both at Wednesbury and Walsal were, however, in bed, so fifty of the mob decided to take Mr Wesley back to his lodging).

. . . But we had not gone a hundred yards when the mob of Walsal came, pouring like a flood, and bore down all before them. The Darlaston mob made what defence they could; but they were weary as well as outnumbered: so that in a short time, many being knocked down, the rest ran away and left me in their hands.

To attempt speaking was vain; for the noise on every side was like the roaring of the sea. So they dragged me along till we came to the town; where, seeing the door of a large house open, I attempted to go in; but a man catching me by the hair, pulled me back into the middle of the mob. They made no more stop till they carried me through the main street, from one end of the town to the other. I continued speaking all the time to those within hearing, feeling no pain or weariness. At the west end of the town, seeing a door half open, I made toward it, and would have gone in; but a gentleman in the shop would not suffer me, saying they would pull the house down to the ground. However, I stood at the door, and asked "Are you willing to hear me speak?" Many cried out, "No, no! Knock his brains out; down with him; kill him at once". Others said "Nay but we will hear him first." I began asking, "What evil have I done? Which of you have I wronged in word or deed?" And continued speaking for above a quarter of an hour till my voice suddenly failed; then the floods began to lift up their voice again; many crying out, "Bring him away! Bring him away!"

In the meantime my strength and my voice returned, and I broke out loud into prayer. And now the man who just before headed the mob, turned and said, "Sir, I will spend my life for you: follow me and not one soul here shall touch a hair of your head". Two or three of his fellows confirmed his words and got close to me immediately. At the same time, the gentleman in the shop cried out, "For shame, for shame! Let him go". An honest butcher who was a little farther off said it was a shame they should do thus; and pulled back four or five, one after another, who were running on the most fiercely. The people then, as it had been by common consent, fell back to the right and left; while those three or four men took me between them, and carried me through them all. But on the bridge the mob rallied again; we therefore went on one side, over the mill dam and thence through the meadows; till, a little before ten, God brought me safe to Wednesbury; having lost only one flap of my waistcoat, and a little skin from one of my hands.

Journal, October 20th, 1743

By what gentle degree does God prepare us for his will! Two years ago a piece of brick grazed my shoulders. It was a year after that the stone struck me between the eyes. Last month I received one blow, and this evening two; one before we came into the town, and one after we were gone out; but both were as nothing; for though one man struck me on the breast with all his might, and the other on the mouth with such force that the blood gushed out immediately, I felt no more pain from either of the blows, than if they had touched me with a straw.

Ibid.

Leisure and I have taken leave of one another. I propose to be busy as long as I live, if my health is so long indulged to me.

Letters Vol. I 34, *to his brother*
Samuel, 5 December 1726

You do not at all understand my manner of life. Though I am always in haste. I am never in a hurry; because I never undertake any more work than I can go through with perfect calmness of spirit. It is true I travel four or five thousand miles in a year. But I generally travel alone in my carriage, and consequently am as retired ten hours a day as if I was in a wilderness. On other days I never spend less than three hours (frequently ten or twelve) in the day alone. Yet I find time to visit the sick and the poor; and I must do it if I believe the Bible, if I believe that these are the marks whereby the Shepherd of Israel will know and judge his sheep at the great day; therefore when there is time and opportunity for it, who can doubt that it is a matter of absolute duty? When I was at Oxford, and lived almost like a hermit, I saw not how any busy man could be saved. I scarce thought it possible for a man to retain the Christian spirit amidst the noise and bustle of the world. God taught me better by my own experience. I had ten times more business in America (that is, at intervals) than ever I had in my life. But it was no hindrance to silence of spirit.

Letters, Vol. VI 292, *to Miss March* 10 December 1777

In riding to Newcastle, I finished the tenth *Iliad* of Homer. What an amazing genius had this man! To write with such strength of thought and beauty of expression, when he had none to go before him! And what a vein of piety runs through his whole work, in spite of his pagan prejudices! Yet one cannot but observe such improprieties intermixed, as are shocking to the last degree.

What excuse can any man of common sense make for "His scolding heroes and his wounded gods"? Nay, does he not introduce even his "father of gods and men," one while shaking heaven with his nod, and soon after using his sister and wife, the empress of heaven, with such language as a carman might be ashamed of? And what can be said for a king, full of days and wisdom, telling Achilles how often he had given him wine, when he was a child and sat in his lap, till he had vomited it up on his clothes? Are these some of those "divine boldnesses which naturally provoke short--sightedness and ignorance to show themselves"?

Journal, Fri. 12th Aug., 1748

6. SOCIETY

Christianity is essentially a social religion. and to turn it into a solitary religion is indeed to destroy it. (By this) I mean not only that (Christianity) cannot subsist so well, but that it cannot subsist at all without society – without living and conversing with other men. But if this be shown, then doubtless, to turn this religion into a solitary one is to destroy it.

Not that we can in anywise condemn the intermixing solitude or retirement with society. This is not only allowable, but expedient; nay, it is necessary, as daily experience shows, for every one that already is, or desires to be, a real Christian. It can hardly be that we should spend one entire day in a continued intercourse with men, without suffering loss in our soul, and in some measure grieving the Holy Spirit of God. We have daily need to retire from the world, at least morning and evening, to converse with God, to commune more freely with our Father which is in secret. Nor indeed can a man of experience condemn even longer seasons of religious retirement, so they do not imply any neglect of the worldly employ wherein the providence of God has placed us.

Works, Vol. V., 296

You seem to apprehend that I believe religion to be inconsistent with cheerfulness and with a sociable, friendly temper. So far from it, that I am convinced, as true religion or holiness cannot be without cheerfulness, so steady cheerfulness, on the other hand, cannot be without holiness or true religion. And I am equally convinced that true religion has nothing sour, austere, unsociable, unfriendly in it; but on the contrary, implies the most winning sweetness, the most amiable softness and gentleness. Are you for having as much cheerfulness as you can? So am I. Do you endeavour to keep alive your taste for all the truly innocent pleasures of life? So do I likewise. Do you refuse no pleasure but what is a hindrance to some greater good or has a tendency to some evil? It is my very rule; and I know no other by which a sincere, reasonable Christian can be guided. In particular, I pursue this rule in eating, which I seldom do without much pleasure. And this I know is the will of God concerning me: that I should enjoy every pleasure that leads to my taking pleasure in him, and in such measure as most leads to it. I know that, as to every action which is naturally pleasing, it is his will that it should be so; therefore, in taking that pleasure so far as it tends to this end (of taking pleasure in God), I do his will. Though, therefore, that pleasure be in some sense distinct from the love of God, yet is the taking of it by no means distinct from his will.

Letters, Vol. I, p. 218

I spent an hour agreeably and profitably with Lady G-H-, and Sir C-H-. It is well a few of the rich and noble are called. Oh that God would increase their number! But I should rejoice (were it the will of God) if it were done by the ministry of others. If I might choose, I should still (as I have done hitherto) preach the gospel to the poor.

Journal, Sat. Nov. 17th 1759

I dined at Lady —. We need great grace to converse with great people! From which therefore, (unless in some rare instance) I am glad to be excused. 'The hours flee away and are put down to our account'. Of these two hours I can give no good account.

Journal, Friday, April 21st, 1758

I left no money to anyone in my will, because I had none. But now considering, that, whenever I am removed, money will soon arise by the sale of books, I added a few legacies by a codicil, to be paid as soon as may be. But I would fain do a little good while I live; for who can tell what will come after him?

Journal, Friday 9th January, 1789

I will not now shock the easiness of your temper by talking about a future state. But suffer me to ask you a question about present things: are you *now* happy?

I have seen a large company of 'reasonable creatures' called Indians sitting in a row on the side of a river, looking sometimes at one another, sometimes at the sky, and sometimes at the bubbles on the water. And so they sat (unless in the time of war) for a great part of the year, from morning to night.

They were doubtless much at ease, but can you think they were happy? And how little happier are you than they?

You eat, and drink, and sleep, and dress, and dance, and sit down to play. You are carried abroad. You are at the masquerade, the theatre, the opera-house, the park, the levee, the drawing-room. What do you do there? Why, sometimes you talk, sometimes you look at one another. And what are you to do tomorrow? The next day? The next week? The next year? You are to eat, and drink, and sleep, and dance, and dress, and play again. And you are to be carried abroad again, that you may again look at one another! And is this all? Alas, how little more happiness have you in this, than the Indians in looking at the sky or water!

Ah poor, dull round! I do not wonder that Col. M— (or any man of reflection) should prefer death itself, even in the midst of his years, to such a life as this, and should frankly declare that he chose to go out of the world because he found nothing in it worth living for.

An Earnest Appeal to Men of
Reason and Religion (1743), 42, 43

Good sort of men do not usually eat to excess; at least, not so far as to make themselves sick with meat, or to intoxicate themselves with drink. And as to the manner of taking it, it is usually innocent, mixed with a little mirth, which is said to help digestion. So far, so good. And provided they take only that measure of plain, cheap, wholesome food, which most promotes health of body and mind, there will be no cause of blame. Neither can I require you to take that advice of Mr. Herbert, though he was a good man:

"Take thy meat; think it dust. Then eat a bit,
And say with all, Earth, to earth I commit."

This is indeed too melancholy; it does not suit with that cheerfulness which is highly proper at a Christian meal. Permit me to illustrate this subject with a little story. The King of France, one day pursuing the chase, outrode all his company, who after seeking him some time, found him sitting in a cottage eating bread and cheeses. Seeing them, he cried out, "Where have I lived all my time? I never before tasted so good food in my life!" "Sire," said one of them, "you never had so good sauce before; for you were never hungry". Now it is true, hunger is a good sauce, but there is one that is better still: that is, thankfulness. Sure, that is the most agreeable food which is seasoned with this. And why not yours at every meal? You need not then fix your eye on death; but receive every morsel as a pledge of eternal life. The Author of your being gives you, in this food, not only a reprieve from death, but an earnest belief that in a little time," death shall be swallowed up in victory."

Works, Vol. VII, 32

I cannot subscribe to (Dr. Cadogan's) condemning of wine in general, several sorts of which, as Dr. Hoffman shows at large, are so far from being unwholesome, that they are some of the most powerful medicines yet known, in some very dangerous diseases. I myself was ordered by Dr. Cheyne (not the warmest advocate for liquors), after drinking only water for some years, to take a small quantity of wine every day. And I am persuaded, far from doing me any hurt, it contributed much to the recovery of my strength. But it seems we are to make a pretty large allowance for what the Doctor says on this head; seeing he grants it will do you little or no harm to take "a plentiful cup now and then". Enough, enough! Then it will certainly do you no harm if, instead of drinking that cup in one day (suppose once a week), you divide it into seven and drink one of them every day.

I cannot but think, if your wine is good in kind, suited to your constitution, and taken in small quantities, it is full as wholesome as any liquor in the world, except water. Yet the grievous abuse of it which almost universally prevails might easily prejudice a benevolent man against it, and make him endeavour to prevent abuse by forbidding the use of it.

Works, Vol. XIV, 280

Our preachers have as great need of temperance in preaching as in eating or drinking; otherwise our grand enemy will carry his point, and soon disable us from preaching at all.

Letters, Vol, VII, 351

We cannot be always intent upon business. Both our bodies and minds require some relaxation. We need intervals of diversion from business. It will be necessary to be very explicit upon this head, as it is a point which has been much misunderstood . . . But I am not obliged to pass any sentence on those that are otherwise minded. I leave them to their own Master. To him let them stand or fall.

Works, Vol. VII, 33

I never myself bought a lottery ticket; but I blame not those that do.

Letters, Vol. VII, 20

That bill was for the share of a lottery ticket. The remaining money you may pay to George Whitefield.

Letters, Vol. VII, 219

I went with two or three friends, to see what are called the electrical experiments. How must these also confound those poor half-thinkers, who will believe nothing but what they can comprehend! Who can comprehend, how fire lives in water, and passes through it more freely than through air? How flame issues out of my finger, real flame, such as sets fire to spirits of wine? How these, and many more as strange phenomena, arise from the turning round a glass globe? It is all mystery: if happily by any means God may hide pride from man!

Journal, Friday, 16th. Oct. 1747

Having procured an apparatus on purpose, I ordered several persons to be electrified, who were ill of various disorders, some of whom found an immediate, some a gradual cure. From this time I appointed, first some hours in every week, and afterwards an hour in every day, wherein any that desired it, might try the virtue of this surprising medicine. Two or three years after, our patients were so numerous that we were obliged to divide them: so part were electrified in Southwark, part at the Foundery, others near St. Paul's, and the rest near the Seven Dials: the same method we have taken ever since; and to this day, while hundreds, perhaps thousands, have received unspeakable good, I have not known one man, woman or child, who has received any hurt thereby: so that when I hear any talk of the danger of being electrified (especially if they are medical men who talk so), I cannot but impute it to great want either of sense or honesty.

Journal, Tuesday, 9th Nov. 1756

To a Soldier

For have soldiers nothing to do with hell? Why, then, is it

73

so often in thy mouth? Dost thou think God does not hear the prayer? And how often hast thou prayed to him to damn thy soul? Is his ear waxed heavy that it cannot hear? I fear thou wilt find it otherwise. For sin is the high road to hell. And have soldiers nothing to do with sin? . . .

But if there were no other hell, thou hast hell enough within thee. An awakened conscience is hell. Pride, envy, wrath, hatred, malice, revenge – what are these but hell upon earth? And how often hast thou tormented in these flames – flames of lust, envy, or proud wrath! Are not these to thy soul, when blown up to the height, as it were a lake of fire, burning with brimstone? Flee away, before the great gulf is fixed; escape, escape for thy life! If thou hast not strength, cry to God, and thou shalt receive power from on high; and he whose name is rightly called Jesus, shall save thee from thy sins.

And why should he not? Has a soldier nothing to do with heaven? God forbid that you should think so! Heaven was designed for you also. God so loved your soul, that he gave his only-begotten Son, that you believing in him might not perish, but have everlasting life. Receive then, the kingdom prepared for you from the foundation of the world! This, this is the time to make it sure; this short uncertain day of life. Arise, and call upon thy God. Call upon the Lamb, who taketh away the sin of the world, to take away thy sins. Believe in him and thou shalt be saved.

Works, Vol. **XI**, 199f.

I think it was about this time that the soldier was executed. For some time I had visited him every day. But when the love of God was shed abroad in his heart, I told him, "Do not expect to see me any more. He who has now begun a good work in your soul will, I doubt not, preserve

74

you to the end. But I believe Satan will separate us for a season". Accordingly, the next day, I was informed that the commanding officer had given strict orders, neither Mr Wesley, nor any of his people should be admitted; for they were all atheists. But did that man die like an atheist? Let my last end be like his!

Journal, March 29th, 1740

Conversation with an attempted suicide

" . . . But, I hear," added he, "you preach to a great number of people every night and morning. Pray, what would you do with them? Whither would you lead them? What religion do you preach? What is it good for?" I replied, I *do* preach to as many as desire to hear, every night and morning. You ask what I would do with them. I would make them virtuous and happy, easy in themselves, and useful to others. Whither would I lead them? To heaven: to God the Judge, the lover of all, and to Jesus the Mediator of the new covenant. What religion do I preach? The religion of love: the law of kindness brought to light by the gospel. What is this good for? To make all who receive it enjoy God and themselves: to make them like God, lovers of all, contented in their lives, and crying out at their death, in calm assurance, "O grave, where is thy victory? . . . Thanks be unto God, who giveth *me* the victory, through *my* Lord Jesus Christ".

An Earnest Appeal to Men of Reason and Religion, para. 19

7. THE BURNING CHARITY

O, grant that nothing in my soul
May dwell but thy pure love alone:
O, may thy love possess me whole,
My joy, my treasure, and my crown.
Strange flames far from my heart remove,
My every act, word, thought, be love.

From the German of Paulus Gerhardt (1606-76)
Poetical Works, Vol. I, p. 138

Fire is the symbol of love; and the love of God is the principle and end of all our good works. But truth surpasses figure; and the fire of divine love has this advantage over material fire that it can re-ascend to its source, and raise thither with it all the good works which it produces. And by this means it prevents their being corrupted by pride, vanity, or any evil mixture. But this cannot be done otherwise than by making these good works in a spiritual manner die in God by a deep gratitude, which plunges the soul in him as in an abyss, with all that it is, and all the grace and works for which it is indebted to him; a gratitude whereby the soul seems to empty itself of them, that they may return to their source, as rivers seem willing to empty themselves, when they pour themselves with all their waters into the sea.

Works, Vol. XI, p. 441

Charity cannot be practised right, unless, First, we exercise it the moment God gives the occasion; and, Secondly, retire the instant after to offer it to God by humble thanksgiving. And this for three reasons: First, to render Him what we have received from Him. The Second, to avoid the dangerous temptation which springs from the very goodness of these works. And the Third, to unite ourselves to God, in whom the soul expands itself in prayer, with all the graces we have received, and the good works we have done, to draw from Him new strength against the bad effects which these very works may produce in us, if we do not make use of the antidotes which God has ordained against these poisons. The true means to be filled anew with the riches of grace is thus to strip ourselves of it; and without this it is extremely difficult not to grow faint in the practice of good works.

Works, Vol. XI, p. 436

A Prayer for the Love of God

I know, O Lord, that thou has commanded me, and therefore it is my duty, to love Thee with all my heart, and with all my strength. I know Thou art infinitely holy and overflowing in all perfection; and therefore it is my duty so to love Thee.

I know Thou hast created me, and that I have neither being nor blessing but what is the effect of Thy power and goodness.

I know Thou art the end for which I was created, and that I can expect no happiness but in Thee.

I know that in love to me, being lost in sin, thou didst

send Thy only Son, and that He, being the Lord of glory, did humble Himself to the death upon the cross, that I might be raised to glory.

I know Thou hast provided me with all necessary helps for carrying me through this life to that eternal glory, and this out of the excess of Thy pure mercy to me, unworthy of all mercies.

I know Thou hast promised to be Thyself my 'exceeding great reward;' though it is Thou alone who Thyself 'workest in me, both to will and to do of Thy good pleasure.'

Upon these, and many other titles, I confess it is my duty to love Thee, my God, with all my heart. Give Thy strength unto Thy servant, that Thy love may fill my heart, and be the motive of all the use I make of my understanding, my affections, my senses, my health, my time, and whatever other talents I have received from Thee. Let this, O God, rule my heart without a rival; let it dispose all my thoughts, words, and works; and thus only can I fulfil my duty and Thy command, of loving Thee 'with all my heart, and mind, and soul, and strength.'

A Collection of Forms of Prayer for every day in the week (first printed 1733), *Works,* Vol. XI, pp. 204-5

Letter to William Wilberforce

My dear Sir – Unless the Divine power has raised you up to be as *Athanasius contra mundum,* I see not how you can go through your glorious enterprise, in opposing that villainy which is the scandal of religion, of England and of human nature. Unless God has raised you up for this very thing, you will be worn out by the opposition of men and devils. But if God be for you who can be against you? Are all of them together stronger than God? O, be not weary of well doing! Go on, in the name of God, and in the power of his might, till even American slavery (the vilest that ever saw the sun) shall vanish before it.

Reading this morning a tract wrote by a poor African, I was particularly struck by that circumstance, that a man who has a black skin, being wronged or outraged by a white man, can have no redress; it being a *law* in our colonies that the *oath* of a black against a white goes for nothing. What villainy is this! That he who has guided you from youth up may continue to strengthen you in this and all things is the prayer of, dear Sir,

Your affectionate servant
Letters Vol. VIII, 265, February 24th, 1791

BIBLIOGRAPHY

Albert C. Outler (ed.) John Wesley (Library of Protestant
  Thought, Oxford 1964)

V. H. H. Green, *The Young Mr Wesley* (London 1961)

Martin Schmidt, *John Wesley,* A Theological Biography translated
  by Norman P. Goldhawk Vols. I and II (London 1962 and
  1971)

R. E. Davies and E. G. Rupp (ed.) *A History of the Methodist Church
  in Great Britain* (Vol. I, 1966)

G. Elsie Harrison, *Son to Susanna* (London 1937)

R. Newton Flew, *The Idea of Perfection in Christian Theology* (Oxford
  1934)